# Countries of the World

# China

by Michael Dahl

**Content Consultant:**
Grace Feng
Member of the Chinese American Library Association

# Bridgestone Books

an imprint of Capstone Press

Bridgestone Books are published by Capstone Press
818 North Willow Street, Mankato, Minnesota 56001
http://www.capstone-press.com

*Library of Congress Cataloging-in-Publication Data*
Dahl, Michael S.
    China/by Michael Dahl.
    p. cm.--(Countries of the world)
    Includes bibliographical references and index.
    Summary: An introduction to the geography, history, economy,
culture, and people of China, the third largest country in the world.
    ISBN 1-56065-566-6
    1. China--Juvenile literature.   [1. China.]  I. Title.
II. Series: Countries of the world (Mankato, Minn.)
DS706.D28    1998
951--dc21

                                        97-5495
                                        CIP
                                        AC

Photo credits
Jean Buldain, cover, 14, 16
Michele Burgess, 18
Capstone Press, 5 (left)
Betty Crowell, 6, 12, 20
International Stock/Jeremy Scott, 5 (right)
Unicorn/Jeff Greenberg, 8; Florent Flipper, 10

# Table of Contents

# Fast Facts

**Name:** People's Republic of China
**Capital:** Beijing
**Population:** More than 1 billion
**Language:** Mandarin
**Religions:** Buddhism, Taoism
  *Most Chinese people are atheists.*

**Size:** 3,696,100 square miles
  (9,609,900 square kilometers)
  *China is slightly larger than the
  United States.*
**Main Crops:** Rice, tea, and wheat

## Maps

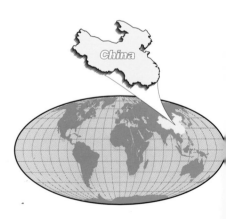

4

## Flag

China's flag is red. Red stands for Communism. Communism is a way of ruling a country. The flag has a large yellow star in its upper left corner. Four small stars are curved around the large star. These stars stand for the five different parts of China.

## Currency

China's unit of currency is the Yuan.

*It takes more than eight Yuan to equal one U.S. dollar.*

# A Giant Country

China is the third largest country in the world. Only Russia and Canada are larger. China has more people than any other country. More than 1 billion people live there. Most people live in eastern China.

Much of China is covered by mountains or deserts. The Himalayas are part of China. The Himalayas are the world's highest mountains.

Water covers parts of China, too. The Chang Jiang is the world's second largest river. Farmers grow rice, potatoes, and cotton along its banks.

People have lived in China for thousands of years. Chinese people have made many important discoveries. One Chinese ruler made cloth from the silk of silkworms. Some Chinese people invented paper and printing. Others invented spaghetti and ice cream. Sunglasses and fireworks are Chinese inventions, too.

China has several mountain ranges.

# Life at Home

Many Chinese people live in large cities. They have either apartments or houses. Houses in cities are like North American houses. But Chinese apartments are different. Families in apartments usually share kitchens and bathrooms with others.

Most Chinese people live in the country. Some live in small villages. Houses in villages are usually made of mud or clay. Sometimes Chinese people use stone bricks. Many country houses do not have power or running water.

Most Chinese people rise early in the morning. They exercise before work. People usually travel on bicycles or motor scooters.

China is a crowded country. The government wants each family to have only one child. The government rewards these families. Many Chinese children grow up without brothers or sisters.

**Chinese people usually travel by bicycle.**

9

# Going to School

Most Chinese children begin school at age four. There are many kindergartens in large cities. Schools are open six days a week. Classes begin early in the morning. There are no school buses in China. Children walk or ride bicycles to school.

The Chinese language does not have an alphabet. Instead, different characters stand for words and ideas. There are more than 50,000 characters. Chinese children learn to write many characters in school. Many also learn English.

Students receive two vacations each year. They receive one month of vacation in the winter. They have another month of vacation in the summer.

Older students spend two weeks every year helping the community. They might clean schools or plant trees. Country schools close when it is time to gather crops. That way students can help gather crops, too.

Chinese schools are open six days a week.

# Chinese Food

Rice is the main food of people in southern China. Southern Chinese people eat fish, too. Shark fin soup is a special southern food.

People in northern China eat different foods. They usually eat bread and noodles instead of rice. They like stew and roasts. Peking Duck is one of their special foods.

All Chinese people eat a lot of vegetables. Tea is served with every meal. Most people eat with spoons and chopsticks. Chopsticks are thin sticks used for eating food.

For breakfast, children drink milk made from soybeans. After school, children snack on dried fruits and seeds. Dried cherries and watermelon seeds are favorites.

Sometimes popcorn men visit small villages. They make popcorn for people. Children bring handfuls of corn. The popcorn men heat the corn in a metal pot until it pops.

**Most Chinese people eat with chopsticks.**

# Animals of China

Many kinds of animals live in China. Tigers and leopards live in China's northern forests. Monkeys and elephants live in the jungles. Camels carry people across Chinese deserts.

Chinese farmers raise ducks and geese. They also raise chickens and pigs. Water buffalo help farmers plow their fields. Yaks pull heavy carts in the mountains. A yak is a kind of ox. It is used as a work animal.

Giant pandas live in China, too. China is the only place giant pandas live in the wild. Pandas eat bamboo. Bamboo is a plant. It has a hard stem with nothing inside of it. The Chinese government keeps bamboo forests safe. This helps keep the pandas alive.

China gave the United States two giant pandas in 1972. The pandas live in the national zoo in Washington, D.C.

**Giant pandas live in China.**

# The Great Wall

Long ago, powerful emperors were in charge of China. An emperor is a man who rules a country. One emperor wanted to keep enemies out of northern China. He decided to build a wall to keep them out.

The emperor's workers started building walls. People built walls even after the emperor died. It took hundreds of years to make all the walls. Then the walls were joined together. This made one large wall. The large wall is called the Great Wall. It is still standing today. Thousands of people visit the Great Wall every year.

The Great Wall twists and turns. It is about 1,500 miles (2,400 kilometers) long. It is the longest object ever built. People can even see the Great Wall from space.

The top of the wall is special, too. It is very wide. Five horses could ride side by side on it. Today, visitors can walk on top of the wall.

Visitors can walk on top of the Great Wall.

# Beijing

Beijing (bay-ZHING) is the capital city of China. It is also called Peking (PAY-king). It is the second largest city in China. More than 10 million people live in Beijing. The president of China also lives there.

Beijing has been a city for more than 3,000 years. Some of its old buildings are still standing. New buildings are built next to the old ones.

The Forbidden City is inside Beijing. Emperors once lived there. The Forbidden City is surrounded by a wall. In the past, nothing could be built higher than the wall.

Yellow was a special color in the past. It could only be used by emperors. Buildings in the Forbidden City have yellow roofs.

Today, the Forbidden City is a museum. It is called the Palace Museum. Many people visit it each year.

**Buildings in the Forbidden City have yellow roofs.**

# Chinese Sports

Most people in China enjoy exercise and sports. Chinese students learn to play basketball and volleyball in school. Some Chinese athletes are famous divers and swimmers. Athletes are people who play sports. Chinese athletes have also done well in volleyball and basketball.

Ping-pong is another favorite Chinese game. Some parks have outdoor ping-pong tables. That way everyone can play the game.

Many people take part in early morning exercises. They do the exercises as a group. These exercises are done on the streets or in parks.

Many Chinese people also practice a martial art. A martial art is a way of fighting or defending oneself. Wushu (WOO-shoo) is the name for all Chinese martial arts. Some Chinese people practice wushu just for exercise. Others practice wushu because it has special meaning for them.

**Many people do morning exercises in parks.**

# Hands On: Play Dancing Dragon

The Chinese believe that the dragon stands for good luck. Many Chinese welcome the New Year with a parade. A dancing dragon is a favorite feature of the parade. You can play dancing dragon, too.

## What You Need

Eight or more players
A large playing area

## What You Do

1. Choose a leader for the dance. The other players should line up behind that person. They should put their hands on the shoulders of the person in front of them.
2. The first person in line is the dragon's head. The last person in line is the dragon's tail.
3. The tail starts the game. The tail shouts, "1, 2, 3, dragon!"
4. Then everyone begins to run. The head leads the line. The head tries to catch the tail. If the head tags the tail, the head earns a point.
5. If the line breaks, the dragon dies. Then the head moves to the back of the line. The head becomes the tail. The next person in line becomes the new head.
6. The player with the most points wins.

## Learn to Speak Mandarin Chinese

| | | |
|---|---|---|
| **good day** | wu an | (OO AHN) |
| **good evening** | wan shàng hao | (WAHN SHUNG HOW) |
| **good morning** | zao chén hao | (ZOW CHEN HOW) |
| **good night** | wan an | (WAHN AHN) |
| **hello** | ni hao | (NEE HOW) |
| **see you again** | zài jiàn | (ZEYE JEE-en) |
| **see you next time** | zài hùi | (ZEYE HWAY) |
| **see you tomorrow** | míng tian jiàn | (MEENG KIN JEN) |
| **thank you** | xiè xiè | (SHEE SHEE) |

## Words to Know

**chopsticks** (CHOP-sticks)—two equal-length thin sticks used for eating food

**emperor** (EM-pur-ur)—a man who rules a country

**martial art** (MAR-shuhl ART)—a way of defending oneself or fighting

**wushu** (WOO-shoo)—the name for all Chinese martial arts

**yak** (YAK)—a kind of ox that is used as a work animal

## Read More

**Haskins, Jim**. *Count Your Way Through China*.
Minneapolis: Carolrhoda Books, 1990.

**Jacobsen, Karen**. *China*. Chicago: Children's Press, 1990.

## Useful Addresses and Internet Sites

**Embassy of the People's Republic of China**
2300 Connecticut Avenue
Washington, DC  20008

**China National Tourist Office**
333 West Broadway, Suite 201
Glendale, CA  91204

**China Today**    http://www.chinatoday.com

**Made in China**    http://china.utopia.com

## Index